For our loving dog, Ghost, who thinks all
bouncing spheres belong to him.

—E.E.

To the love of my life, thank you for
making me smile every single day.

—A.L.

Spheres All Year
Hardcover first edition • June 2023 • ISBN: 978-1-958629-22-2
Paperback first edition • June 2023 • ISBN: 978-1-958629-21-5
eBook first edition • June 2023 • ISBN: 978-1-958629-18-5

Written by Elizabeth Everett, Text © 2023
Illustrated by Anuki López, Illustrations © 2023

Project Manager, Cover and Book Design: Caitlin Burnham
Editors: Marlee Brooks and Hannah Thelen
Editorial Assistants: Liliann Albelbaisi, Emilee Rae Hibshman, and Chloe Cattaneo

Available in bilingual English/Spanish as Spheres All Year / Esferas todo el año
Paperback first edition • June 2023 • ISBN: 978-1-958629-23-9
Board Book first edition • June 2023 • ISBN: 978-1-958629-17-8
eBook first edition • June 2023 • ISBN: 978-1-958629-20-8

Teacher's Guide available at the Educational Resources page of ScienceNaturally.com.

Published by:
    Science, Naturally! — An imprint of Platypus Media, LLC
    750 First Street NE, Suite 700
    Washington, DC 20002
    202-465-4798 • Fax: 202-558-2132
    Info@ScienceNaturally.com • ScienceNaturally.com

Distributed to the book trade by:
    National Book Network (North America)
        301-459-3366 • Toll-free: 800-462-6420
        CustomerCare@NBNbooks.com • NBNbooks.com
    NBN International (worldwide)
        NBNi.Cservs@IngramContent.com • Distribution.NBNi.co.uk

Library of Congress Control Number: 2022948134

10 9 8 7 6 5 4 3 2 1

SPHERES ALL YEAR

Written by Elizabeth Everett

Illustrated by Anuki López

Science, Naturally!
An imprint of Platypus Media, LLC
Washington, D.C.

**Spheres are round just like a ball—
they have no points or corners at all.**

Not flat like a circle, a sphere you can hold.
Across the ground, they can be rolled.

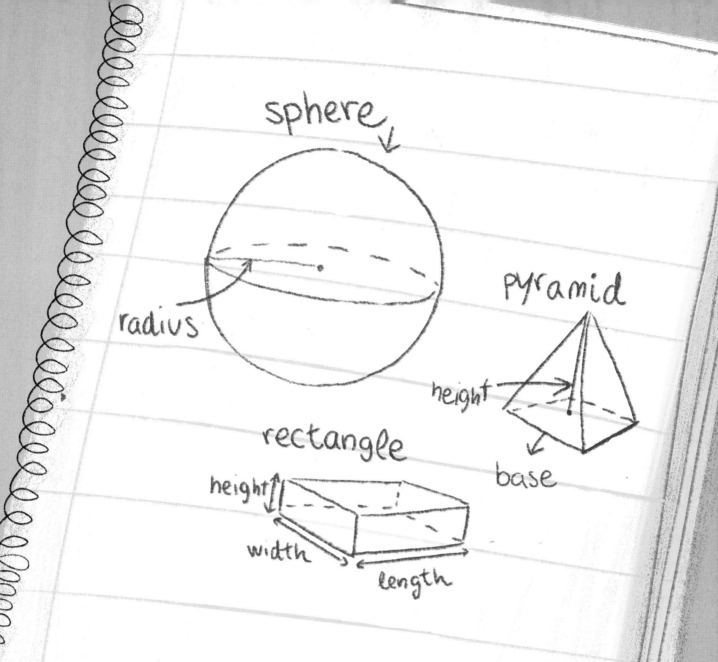

To make a sphere, three dimensions unite:
these 3-D objects have length, width, and height.

Look all around you and it will be clear,
there are so many different kinds of spheres!

**Summer, fall, winter, and spring:
discover the spheres each season will bring!**

Big scoops of ice cream taste just right,
cooling us off in the warm sunlight.

Turtle eggs hatch in their underground nest.
The moon will guide them, there's no time to rest!

Sweet round cherries with hard pits inside
leave all of our fingertips purple-dyed.

A brightly colored beach ball tossed in the air makes a hot day something special to share.

A soccer ball rolls through freshly cut grass.
The players kick it and shout, "Here, pass!"

Soon orange pumpkins grow all around,
and bright red leaves crunch on the ground.

Warm sugared donuts make quite a snack
after jumping in leaves and raking them back.

Eating candy as the air gets chilly,
the costumes we see are all so silly!

Walking outside, cold snow starts to fall.
It's time for a hat with a pom-pom ball.

A set of three snowballs, carefully packed,
makes a snow friend, haphazardly stacked.

To finish the year, we roll cookie dough.
We try to be patient, but the oven's so slow!

Outside the window, the full moon is bright
on a long and peaceful starlit night.

The weather warms, green colors abound.
The Sun comes out, shining and round.

A little seed that we plant in the earth
becomes a red radish popping out of the dirt.

Purple flower puffs line the street,
making the air smell fresh and sweet.

Watch sparkling bubbles float away—
what a wonderful way to spend the day!

You've discovered the spheres each season brings,
from summer and fall to winter and spring.

**And don't forget that Earth is a sphere,
where we spend each day, all year!**

Spheres can be as big as the stars that twinkle,
or as teeny tiny as a rainbow sprinkle.

Look around you and it will be clear,
there are so many different kinds of spheres!

What Are 2-D Shapes?

Dimensions are used to measure and describe shapes. They can tell us how long a shape is, how wide, and how high.

Some shapes only have two dimensions, like length and width <u>or</u> height and width. These are called 2-D shapes.

When a shape is 2-D, it is flat. Examples of 2-D shapes include circles, squares, and triangles.

What Are 3-D Shapes?

Some shapes have three dimensions, like length, width, <u>and</u> height. These are called 3-D shapes.

Unlike 2-D shapes, 3-D shapes are never flat. Examples of 3-D shapes include spheres, cubes, and pyramids.

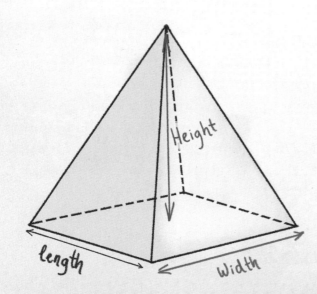

Meet the Author and Illustrator

Elizabeth Everett spent 16 years as a classroom teacher before venturing into writing. She is inspired by her energetic youngster, Jalen, and his love for books. She currently lives in Colorado with her family where they love spending time outdoors in the Western sun. She is the author of *This Is the Sun* and *Twinkle, Twinkle, Daytime Star*. She can be reached at Elizabeth.Everett@ScienceNaturally.com.

Anuki López studied Fine Arts at the University of Seville in Spain. She has been drawing since she can remember; a notebook and colored pencils were her favorite toys. She loves working and living her life as an illustrator, bringing children illustrations that are full of color, magic, humor, animals, respect, and, of course, love. You can see more of her art on her Instagram page, @anukilopez.